Dad,
Than'
your lov
Teressa + Jordon

Contrast Brings Clarity

The Unexpected Path that Led Me to Homeschooling

Teressa Kennedy

Dedication

This book is dedicated to my inspiration, my son Jay. I am so thankful that God entrusted me to be your mother. Raising you has truly given me a sense of purpose far beyond. Through your life, I have learned so many life lessons. I am truly a better person because of you. You have a special gift, and I have no doubt that God will use your gift to accomplish some amazing things in your lifetime.

Love you always,

Mom

Contents

The Backstory
PART I

Chapter 1
In the Beginning

From the time I was a teenager, I always knew I would be a mother someday. I envisioned having a great career in music, and then when the time was right, I would get married and have a daughter. She would be named Kennedy. As I got older, life became more complex, and my decisions led me to take a completely different path. I must say this new path led to many adventures that I would not soon forget. One of them was leaving my family and moving to Michigan. If you were to ask my twenty-one-year-old self why I moved, I would have told you that I did it for love. From where I stand now, I would tell you that God allowed me to move so that I could grow closer to Him. I experienced many God-ordained moments in Michigan, from meeting lifelong friends who have become my extended family to attending graduate school at the

University of Michigan. I made more money than I ever had in my adult career at the then-largest software company in the United States. The icing on the cake was buying my first home in my early twenties.

God continued to show his favor upon me in Michigan. For the first two years, I did not plan on ever moving back to California. However, things began to shift during the fourth year. The economy was hit really hard, and it seemed there was a mass exodus from Michigan. I also began really missing my family and friends back home. Moreover, my love life was not taking shape as I thought it would, and quite frankly, for the first time, I felt very uncertain about my future. I began spending more time with the Lord, seeking direction for my life. Some months later, two key connections would change my life. First, I reconnected with James, an old friend who I dated in high school. At the time, we were merely two friends catching up. I would find out years later just how life-changing this reconnection had been.

The second connection occurred during one of my many trips to California. It was the winter of 2006, and I remember having a great time visiting friends and family. The afternoon before my flight back to Michigan, I saw a job post in San Francisco that piqued my interest. Not thinking much of it, I submitted my resume. To my surprise, the director responded a few hours later, requesting an in-person interview! My thoughts were moving at a hundred miles per hour. I had no idea what I was going to do. Finally, after calming down, I replied, letting her know that I lived in Michigan and was only available to meet with her the following day. She agreed, and so I called the airline to change my flight. I would spend the next day interviewing with an executive panel at the university.

That day set me on a new course. When I got on the plane, I knew that position was earmarked for me and that God was calling me back to California. Within six weeks, I had accepted the job offer, packed up my house, hired a property manager to help rent it out, and had flown back to The Golden State.

When I moved back to California, love was the last thing on my mind. I was solely focused on establishing myself in my new job. Well, for the most part. But, I was also reconnecting with my sister-friends. Oh, we had a great time, and it seemed we had something planned every weekend.

I know by now you're probably thinking, what does any of this have to do with having a child and homeschooling? Well, for me, it had everything to do with the amazing child I was going to birth and the journey I would embark upon once he came into the world. You see, in Michigan, I was separated from my family and friends. But as difficult as this was for me, God used that time to show me that my destiny is not defined by what others may say, but rather my destiny lies in Him. This prompted a season of self-discovery about my purpose, separate from anyone else, and I began seeing myself through His eyes. Once I had learned the lessons I needed to learn in Michigan, God enabled me to return to California renewed and ready to live.

As I settled into my new life, I felt complete. I had an amazing job, wonderful friends, and I was near my family again. What more could I ask for? Little did I know there was a God-ordained moment right around the corner.

It was a sunny but cool Saturday afternoon in early January 2007. I remember sitting in my home office looking out the window, thinking about how tired I was. The previous evening, my mother had been installed as the President of the Lathrop District Chamber of Commerce. It had been a wonderful evening, full of excitement, as my mother was the first African American to receive that honor. Suddenly, I felt this urge to go to the mall and look for picture frames. I hesitated, but eventually, I went. From what I can remember, I had no makeup and was wearing a jogging suit and some clunky sneakers. I walked around the store looking for picture frames, but nothing caught my eye, so I just started walking aimlessly around, looking at clothes. (It always amazes me how much extra time I had before having a child…. But I digress.)

After walking around the store for about thirty minutes, I was ready to go home. Then from out of nowhere, I felt the Spirit of the Lord tell me to go to Target and get detergent. So I thought, okay, I'll drive to Target. Just a quick side note: Target is actually connected to the mall. So I could either walk through the mall or drive to Target. I guess I was being lazy and so I decided to drive. Then the Spirit of the Lord told me to walk. So that is exactly what I did.

My mood was a bit off that day. I just wanted to get my detergent and go home. So what did I do? I pulled out my phone and pretended I was talking to someone as I walked through the mall so that no one would talk to me. I didn't get very far before I saw a gentleman walking toward me, and before I knew it, he had walked up to me and said, "Hello, my name is Joseph. Here is my business card. Give me a call, and we can go to lunch sometime." Forgetting I was pretending to be talking on my phone, I looked at him, and he smiled and said, "How are you?" I do not remember how the rest of the conversation went, but I do remember feeling that I was not very kind to him. I also remember being so proud of my new role at the university that I quickly grabbed my business card from my purse and handed it to him when he gave me his business card. As I walked away from Joseph, I felt conflicted. Perhaps I should not have spoken to him like that.

That was a Saturday afternoon, and for the remainder of the day and throughout Sunday, I thought about him. So I told myself that I would email him and apologize on Monday morning when I went to work. Well, he beat me to it. When I got to the office and logged on to my computer, an email from Joseph popped up. We exchanged phone numbers and talked later that day. All it took was that one phone conversation, and soon we became very close. I knew almost immediately that Joseph was a gift from God. Our season was very short but very meaningful. So much so that when we were around each other, I felt God's love for me embodied in a man. That was a first for me.

Now you may be asking yourself, did it turn into anything more? Although I wanted it to, God had other plans for me. I am sharing this experience with you because that is the moment in my life that opened my heart to receive the unconditional love that was coming my way.

It took about ten months for me to fully accept not having Joseph in my life. The last thing I wanted was to remain mentally, physically, or emotionally stagnant, so I began traveling and connecting with friends. In this season in my life, I still felt blessed being back in California, but now life had more of a serious tone to it. I was no longer a university employee: I was now an independent contractor with a Northern California Community College leadership collaborative. It was a lot of work, but it was also fulfilling. I had always desired to be self-employed, and now that desire was taking shape. Professionally I was doing well, but on a personal level, I lacked direction — and I needed to find one fast (or so I thought).

The first thing I did was to join an awesome church in Oakland. I also started singing again; that alone helped me feel more centered. And then came James…

I mentioned earlier reconnecting with a high school friend I had dated. Well, in early January 2008, a good friend of mine from New York was flying to Los Angeles to attend a music conference, so I told him I'd meet him there. As I was making my arrangements, I contacted other friends who lived in Los Angeles to let them know I would be there for the weekend. One of these was James, my old high school friend. This was one of the first trips where I had no expectations other than getting away and enjoying myself. Well, this trip proved to be life-changing in the most unexpected way.

Chapter 2
A Bouncing Baby Boy

About two weeks after my trip to Los Angeles, I was feeling awful. I was nauseous and unable to keep down what I ate. I thought it was an extreme case of the flu. I remember taking flu medicine, steam baths, and walking around with a heating pad over my stomach — basically anything I could do to feel better. But nothing seemed to help. Then, during one of my store runs, I remember walking down one of the aisles, and the thought hit me: "Am I pregnant?" I immediately pushed the thought aside, or at least I tried. After what felt like twenty minutes of circling the same aisle, I couldn't take it anymore. I grabbed the least expensive pregnancy test I could find (why spend money on a negative test?) and left the store as fast as I could; I would have been so embarrassed if someone I knew had seen what I was buying. When I got home, I took the pregnancy test, expecting it to yield a negative result. But low and behold: it was positive! However, I convinced myself that it was a false positive. I know you're probably thinking: it's time to see a doctor. You're absolutely correct, I should have, but at that time, I was in total denial. As usual, I tried to carry on, hoping I would feel better, but of course, that is not how things played out. God knew how hard-headed I could be, so He sent a message through someone I would listen to.

I still remember it like it was yesterday. It was a weekend evening, and I was sitting on the sofa eating popcorn while watching television. My phone started ringing. I looked down and saw it was my close friend (sister) Angel from Chicago. I always enjoy our girl time. She was one of the first people I met when I moved to Michigan. We instantly became close friends, and twenty years later, our sisterhood remains strong. That night, God used her to send me a direct message, and it was received loud and clear. I do not recall exactly what we were talking about, but right in the middle of our conversation, Angel began telling about a dream she had had the night before. She said something like, "I had a dream that I was in the hospital, and I was pregnant." I thought nothing of it until she said, "I don't know, but it did not feel like it was me." I paused for a brief moment, and then we began chatting about something else.

Then a few minutes later, she said again, "It just did not feel like it was me." This time my ears perked up because it was unusual for Angel to repeat herself. In the pit of my stomach, I knew it was me. God knew I was not listening to my body, but He knew I would listen to my friend. He was going to have her repeat the dream until I took notice.

The very next day, I scheduled an appointment with my OBGYN. Thankfully, I was scheduled for a same-day appointment. Sitting in the hospital room by myself, I began reflecting on my life. So many wonderful things were unfolding in it. How would a child change all that? Would my contract be affected? Would my friends and church family judge me and treat me differently? I could not keep up with all of the thoughts rushing through my mind. All of a sudden, I heard a knock at the door. The look on my doctor's face said it all. In her kind demeanor, she said, "Congratulations, you are four weeks pregnant!" I felt like I was going to pass out. Yet, I kept my composure while she continued talking. Did I hear anything she said? Not really. I left her office a few minutes later. The walk to my car seemed endless. I probably sat in my car for about twenty minutes. I was in shock. Once I had calmed down, I called James and told him that we would be parents.

I waited for a couple of weeks before sharing the news with my inner circle. My mother already sensed that I was pregnant, but never treated me differently. She would make ginger tea, telling me I would feel better soon. That I did. A few weeks later, in fact, something shifted. I woke up, looked in the mirror and said to myself, "I am going to enjoy this pregnancy."

I have mentioned my desire to have a daughter and to name her Kennedy. As I was not married, I came up with another name, Jaylen Nichole. I put her name in my Bible and talked to "her" all the time, rubbing my belly and calling her 'little mama.'

Some of my friends did not share my vision. They felt I was having a boy. Those friends knew no better than I did what I was having, or did they? Around eighteen weeks, I scheduled an appointment to find out the sex of the baby. I was so excited to see an image of my little girl. My mother and stepfather were so kind to go with me to find out the exciting news. Of course, I already knew; this would merely be confirmation. The medical staff was very pleasant, and I remember the ultrasound technician saying, "Relax, Ms. Kennedy, we get to see your baby today!" I did not want to look. I am not sure why, but I was waiting for my mother to confirm that she saw a little girl. The energy in the room changed, and she was silent. The next thing I heard was, "There's your baby Ms. Kennedy!" My mother was still silent, which I found strange. Then the technician told me we were all done.

As we walked out of the office and to the car, my family was still quiet. The only thing my mother said was, "Let's go to lunch." Once we arrived at the restaurant, she finally told me she had something for me. As I was eating my meal, she looked across the table at me and said, "Congratulations, you're having a boy!" I opened the envelope and saw the ultrasound image: he was big enough for me to clearly make out his jewels. I literally cried.

How did I get it wrong? I had actually named my daughter and had continually rubbed my belly while calling my son 'little mama'. I felt so bad. He had always been very active in my belly, but that night he was very still. He was probably thinking, it's about time you stopped calling me 'little mama'.

It took me a couple of days to center myself, but once I had, my little man and I had a great pregnancy. I made sure I surrounded myself with people who loved me unconditionally, and I believed he could feel that love as well. I also focused on the awesome contract opportunity: I wanted to be a sponge and learn as much as I could from the community college leadership collaborative.

The weeks flew by. I remember being very close to my due date and having to put on a workshop. I wanted to make a great impression, so I prayed that I would not go into labor until after the event. As a side note, I did not tell any of my contractors that I was pregnant. I wanted our interactions to be about the work ahead of us rather than about my pregnancy. I'm happy to say that the event was a big success.

The Lord had placed in my spirit that I should pack my bags on October 4 and stay with my parents until my son was born. My due date was October 8, so he could be born any day. I went to the salon, got my hair done, and then drove to my parents' home. The next evening, my mother brought home a Mexican meal. I do not recall the exact meal, but I remember requesting mango salsa.

As I was enjoying my mango salsa, I started feeling sharp pains in my stomach. At first, I thought it was because the salsa was spicy, but I ruled that out when the pain persisted. I looked at my mom and told her that I thought I was in labor. She suggested I relax and call my doctor. So I tried to relax and talked to the doctor. I was fine for a few hours — until I couldn't take the pain any longer. So we made the sixty-mile trip to the hospital, only to be sent back home. My mom was my partner the entire time. After three trips to the hospital and thirty-six hours of labor, my precious boy Jay was born on October 8. Right on his due date.

My Journey to Non-Traditional Education

PART II

Chapter 3
Unchartered Territory

I remember that during the first three weeks after Jay's birth, I was so nervous about being at home alone with him. He was so little, and I had no clue what I was doing. Thankfully, my parents opened their home to us, and we stayed there for three weeks.

As an entrepreneur, I knew I needed help at home while I worked and met with clients. When I was about eight months pregnant, I began praying to God to send us someone special to help out. I cannot begin to tell how God exceeded my expectations and blessed us with a wonderful caregiver. I never told Jay's caregiver, but it was thanks to her that I was able to go back home as soon as I did. Her help enabled me to work from home and meet with clients.

When Jay was nearing two years old, I was given a great opportunity to work with a major company in Oakland. It all made sense on paper: it was a prestigious role, with a great benefits package for Jay and me, and I could continue to work my business on the side. Once I accepted my new role, I worked on a transition plan with my son's caregiver and began looking for a preschool. Fortunately, it did not take long for me to find a wonderful preschool near our home. Everything was falling into place. Surely this must be the next step in our journey, right?

Well, not quite. There were two things I had failed to consider. First, I had not taken into account how my son would deal with the transition. He had been home full time for two years, and now he would be at a preschool full time. Second, and most important, I had not taken the time to ask God if that was the right opportunity for us. I truly wish I had.

For the most part, Jay was healthy. Occasionally he would catch a minor cold, but within a few days, he was back to his bubbly self. When he turned two, however, our world shifted. Within the first two weeks of being at the preschool, Jay was constantly sick. It felt like I was taking him to the Emergency Room at least twice a month. My poor baby had terrible sinus infections, constant drainage, and on occasion, bronchitis. Things got so bad that he would hold his breath at night. Needless to say, I let Jay sleep in my bed so that I could monitor his condition. It wasn't easy, but I did my best to juggle my new position and take care of my little boy. I just wanted my son to feel better.

As wonderful as it looked on paper, I began feeling that this situation was not the role God wanted me to take. That was confirmed when I received a call from my son's preschool telling me he had refused to take off his jacket and did not want anyone to touch him. Jay had gone from being a happy, joyful little boy to being unhappy and uncommunicative with his teachers and peers. The following day, I gave my two weeks notice. As soon as I did, I felt like a huge burden had been removed.

I was not making as much money, but Jay and I were happier. However, that did not solve his sinus challenges. We spent many of our days (or it seemed) at the doctor's office. My son was prescribed a number of nasal sprays to try and shrink his membranes. Honestly, I never felt comfortable with that procedure. Jay was only two years old and the nasal sprays, I felt, were too strong. Most importantly, he did not like using those nasal sprays one bit.

Around Jay's third birthday, I made an appointment with an ENT specialist in Oakland. The otolaryngologist was a very nice man. It took him only a few minutes to determine what was causing my son's sinus infections: Jay had enlarged adenoids, and fluid lodged in his ears. Without hesitation, he told me he was a practicing physician at Children's Hospital in Oakland and could schedule Jay for surgery within the next three weeks. I should mention here that three months earlier, I had tried to schedule an appointment with an otolaryngologist only to be informed that there was a one-year waiting list! But now, my son would actually get the relief he needed in only three weeks. So we were destined to meet this particular specialist.

The surgery went very well. I was a ball of nerves, but Jay was so brave. As he recovered, I could see my happy little boy come back to me. It was amazing. Over the next few months, Jay's appetite increased, his sinus infections went away, he had a growth spurt, and he was much more communicative. However, there were also a few disadvantages. After the fluid was drained from his ears, my son became very sensitive to noise. Sounds like a motorcycle or a fire engine were overwhelming for him. Also, he spoke with what seemed like an accent, almost like a New Yorker accent. To this day, I still do not understand how that happened.

Things in our lives were going so well that I decided to enroll Jay in a different preschool near our home. This experience was very different for my son but in a positive way. The teachers were very kind and welcoming, and there was a large, grassy area where the kids could play. As my son loved to run, he was thrilled. It seemed like Jay fit right in. Every day, when I came to pick him up, I was greeted at the door and debriefed about his day. I really felt that he was in a nurturing environment.

Shortly after Jay turned four, I noticed that his friends were moving into the next group to begin preparing them for kindergarten. When I asked why my son was still in the younger class, I was told that he enjoyed being there and that this would also give him more time to fully potty train. I did not push the issue initially, but I felt that he was getting to an age where he needed to be in the older class. So I scheduled a meeting with the director and his teacher to establish a plan to make sure Jay was prepared for kindergarten.

The first few minutes were very cordial, but what I heard next surprised me. The director proceeded to tell me that Jay did not talk during the course of the day. Furthermore, when he did speak, he would only say one word instead of a full sentence. So they recommended that I have him evaluated to assess any speech and language delays. I remember feeling so disappointed and frustrated, not so much because of that information, but because I hadn't been informed earlier and could have been proactive. I could not help but wonder how long the preschool would have kept Jay in the younger class without saying anything to me about Jay's speech issues.

As I left the room, I knew I had to come up with a plan of action for my son. That night, I prayed about it and asked the Lord for wisdom. A few days later, the Lord provided me with the exact steps I needed to take. I posted an ad on Craigslist seeking a preschool teacher who would be willing to work in our home on a part-time basis during the week. Almost immediately, replies came in. A few were very sketchy, but there was one response that stood out among the rest. Sky was a former preschool teacher with a daughter around the same age as Jay. After calling her references, I invited Sky to our home, and we clicked immediately. We established a start date, which I used to inform the preschool that Jay would now be attending only part-time. This way, it would not cost me anything extra to have a preschool teacher at home and at the facility.

With Sky, everything changed for us. Within two weeks, she had potty trained Jay using techno instrumental music. She was so creative that Jay looked forward to learning something new with her every day. And this enthusiasm translated over to the preschool facility. I remember walking in to pick up Jay one afternoon, and the teacher in the older class smiled at me and said, "Your son is talking." Jay could not tell time yet, but he knew that mom was coming to get him before nap time. Things had greatly improved, and I could see the love of learning and exploring in my son's eyes. But there was still one unanswered question: Did my son have a speech disorder?

I scheduled an appointment to have a speech pathologist evaluate Jay. I was very nervous, but I wanted to know for the sake of my son. Jay did not know he was being evaluated; he thought he was just chatting with the nice lady. And I did not know Jay was also being evaluated for autism. The evaluation lasted approximately forty-five minutes. After the assessment, the pathologist told me that Jay did not have a learning disability but would require mild speech therapy to help him verbalize his thoughts.

With this additional information, I felt that I had a complete picture of what Jay needed for a strong start academically. I sat down with Sky and asked her if she would be willing to work with Jay full time to help him prepare for transitional kindergarten. She agreed, and I withdrew Jay from the preschool.

I planned to have Sky work with Jay for the remainder of the school year. Then I would enroll him in transitional kindergarten at the local school in our district, where he would begin speech therapy. That was my plan.

However, as you've probably gathered by now, my plans for my son are usually not the same ones God has for him.

Chapter 4
Let's Make This Official

Things were going very well with Sky. She incorporated math, science, language, and historical elements into Jay's lesson plans each week. As a teacher, she was so creative. For example, a simple but fun science project they worked on (we still have it) was an oil, water, and food coloring science experiment. I remember Jay being so amused that oil and water did not mix. Sky explained why they didn't, and he took it all in like a sponge. Although I worked with Jay on the alphabet and words associated with each letter, Sky's creative abilities made mastering the alphabet exciting.

Sometimes I would peek in the living room and listen in on the lesson. It filled my heart with such joy. It showed me that learning should be fun, especially at that age. As a child, my own experiences were not focused on the process of learning but more on the results. I never told my parents, but in the third grade, I felt like a fish out of water. I struggled with math concepts, and I dreaded being in the classroom and having the teacher pick me to answer a question or solve a math problem. Interestingly enough, I still earned good grades that year. I worked hard in school because I was well aware of the expectations my parents had for me. I still remember how that little girl felt. Maybe that is why I was so sensitive to Jay's learning experience.

Toward the end of the school year, I made an appointment to meet with the speech therapist, and transitional kindergarten teacher at the school Jay would be attending. Upon entering the school, I was greeted by the speech therapist; she walked me to an office where we began to chat. Once I sat down, a woman walked in and introduced herself. She was going to be Jay's teacher next year. We went over my son's speech and language evaluation results and discussed how he would transition from classroom instruction to speech therapy during the week. With the three of us helping out, I felt that Jay would have the support he needed. As I stood up, I asked one final question: What was the teacher-to-student ratio? The teacher told me there were twenty-eight students to one teacher and one aide. I thanked them both, shook their hands, and left the office. As I walked down the hall, I thought, "That's a lot of kids in one classroom...."

When I got home, Jay was just finishing his school day. My mind was racing with a hundred questions. Would he flourish in a classroom with twenty-seven other children? Would he feel comfortable asking his teacher for help if he did not understand something? How would he handle being in one classroom for four to five hours? Is he prepared for transitional kindergarten? As I was pondering all of these questions, Sky walked right past me, and I thought, "Why not ask her?" So I did. "I don't think he is ready yet," she replied. We both felt the same way.

So now I had a decision to make. Do I keep Jay learning at home for an additional year, or do I move forward and enroll him in the local school? Those of you who thought I would select the latter are getting a good sense of my personality. I'm a planner, so I was determined to stick with the plan. Together, to the best of our ability, Sky and I worked on a plan over the summer to help prepare Jay for school.

I began doing some research on my own about non-traditional teaching methods. Although I am not a teacher, I felt confident that I could help teach Jay. As I was looking for creative ways to add to what Sky was already teaching him, my childhood friend Trisha from church came to mind out of the blue. I had not spoken with her in many years, but I remembered that she homeschooled her children. As soon as I thought about her, I felt a sense of relief and immediately messaged her on Facebook.

We connected about a week later and had a great conversation. I had so many questions to ask her, given her homeschooling experience. However, with my first question, the conversation took a completely different turn. I inquired about resources for preparing a child for transitional kindergarten. As Trisha shared some online resources I could use, she stopped mid-sentence and informed me that she was an Educational Specialist with a local virtual online charter school. If I were interested in homeschooling, she told me, I could apply to her charter school, and she would request to have Jay placed on her roster.

I did not know what to think or how to feel. I'm sure Trisha could sense that, so she told me to take some time to think about it — but not too much time: the application window would close in one week. As I recall it all now, I realize the Lord was not giving me much time because he knew I would try to stick to my plan.

The next day, I met with Sky after she had completed her lesson for the day. I have to admit, I was a little nervous about talking to her. For me, it was about perception. Even though I was scattered, I didn't want to appear that way. What was supposed to be a quick conversation turned into a pretty lengthy one. Thankfully, Sky was willing to partner with me and help with the teaching if I chose to homeschool Jay.

That night I did not sleep very well. I thought I had everything planned out, but now I was not so sure. I asked the Lord what would be the best decision for Jay and eventually fell asleep. I woke up the next morning with this question in my head: "Who do you trust?" I laid in the bed and, as I pondered, more questions arose: Who do I trust to help me with my son's education? Do I trust the local school? Do I trust Trisha, who works at the charter school and is willing to place my son on her roster? My response to the first part of the initial question was, I trust God, and I trust that my friend from the church will look after my son as if he were her own child. (Yes, I was actually having a conversation with myself).

Without any further hesitation, I completed the online application for the charter school, and just like that, our lives shifted in another direction. This time, however, I felt more confident because I had my son's in-home teacher working alongside managing the process and because I would still be able to work with my clients.

Things seemed to be going smoothly as I excitedly began preparing for the start of the school year. I was busily ordering school supplies for the house, a new desk, and anything else I could think of that would make Jay's learning experience a positive one.

I remember we were only two weeks away from the beginning of school. I was taking a nap when my phone rang. It was Sky. I could feel that something was different. When I answered, she told me that her daughter was not feeling well, so she would not be able to work with Jay that day. I told her that I completely understood and would see her tomorrow. Well, the next morning, Sky called to let me know her daughter was in fact very ill and that they were taking her to the hospital: after running many tests over the last few weeks, the doctor had diagnosed her daughter with leukemia. My heart broke for her and Sky. We both knew that this meant the end of our working relationship because Sky would now have to fight for her daughter's health.

I hung up the phone completely numb. Jay would be starting school soon, and I now had no one to help me teach him while I was working. I remembered thinking: What in the world am I going to do now?!

Chapter 5
You Said What?

Jay was four days away from starting transitional kindergarten, and I felt so alone. I think I spent two of those four days sulking and feeling sorry for myself. But something shifted the third day because I woke up feeling very positive. I said out loud, "You can do this!" That day I organized Jay's learning area and my own workspace. My sadness was replaced with a feeling of excitement. Naively, I felt that all my son needed was one-on-one instruction, and he would grasp the material and flourish quickly.

The first day of school arrived. I woke up super early, expecting the day to feel different as if someone would magically schedule Jay's day for us so I would know where to begin. Should I start with math first? Or read a story? I had no clue where to begin, so we read a book and worked on tracing some letters. Jay was so happy to spend the day with me, but I was feeling completely off-kilter.

I quickly learned that I needed to draw up a schedule to help keep me on track and feel as if we were making progress each day. Based upon my client meetings throughout the week, I put together a homeschooling schedule similar to this one:

- 8:30 am – Breakfast
- 10:00 am – Math
- 10:15 am – Phonics
- 10:45 am – Reading
- 11:00 am – Handwriting
- 11:15 am – Science

Once I had a schedule, our daily routine really improved, and at the end of each day, I felt that Jay had learned something new. The schedule also calmed my nerves because now I had a framework to help me manage both my workload and homeschooling. It also helped Jay because it set the expectation for each day.

Every twenty days, one is required to have an in-person meeting with the Educational Specialist (E.S.) assigned to one's child. I was so thrilled that Jay's E.S. was a family friend. Between the two of us, we were going to ensure that Jay would thrive. I was very thankful to have an accountability partner again to advise me in homeschooling Jay.

Our first in-person meeting with Trisha was in early September 2013. We decided to meet at a location equidistant from our homes. With my parents' approval, we decided to hold our meetings at their home. As I was pulling into their driveway, I could see Trisha in the rearview mirror. Excited, I hurried to park and got out of the car to greet her. We walked in the front door together, briefly catching up on old times.

We sat at the dining room table, and I introduced Jay to Trisha. From what I remember, Jay probably said hello, and that was the extent of their conversation. What I was not prepared for, and perhaps should have been, is that Jay would rarely speak to Trisha at any of our meetings, occasionally responding with one- or two-word answers. I thought to myself, here we go again. What my son did not realize is that his lack of communication made it more challenging for Trisha to form a solid assessment of his progress. As soon as she left, however, he would start talking to his grandparents and me. There were times when I was embarrassed, but on the plus side, as Trisha was a mother herself, she knew how to get Jay to let his guard down to obtain the information she needed to report back to the charter school. Also, as Jay had an IEP for speech through the school, he attended two thirty-minute therapy sessions per week, so I thought this might help him open up more.

Jay and I continued to make progress throughout the school year, and my confidence began to grow. I really started believing that I could manage both homeschooling and work. Thankfully, I did have help. When I had a client meeting, a babysitter or my parents would watch Jay for me.

In what seemed like the blink of an eye, the end of the school year arrived. We'd made it! Jay had one last official learning period meeting with Trisha. This one would be slightly different in that she was going to administer an assessment to capture Jay's growth over the course of the school year. With all of the work we had put into this year, I knew Jay was ready.

The morning of our meeting with Trisha, I was excited. Jay and I drove to the school's Learning Center, about thirty miles away. When we walked into the building, there were students in various areas of the center. Some were meeting with their E.S. or taking an in-person class. I could tell Jay was taking in all of the sights and sounds around him. Within five minutes, Trisha walked up to us and escorted us back to one of the empty tables. After we debriefed about his work samples, Trisha explained to Jay what would take place during the assessment. As this was a transitional kindergarten, a parent could be present during the assessment. Trisha pulled out the master test scantron and laid it on the table. "Are you ready?" she asked. Jay nodded. I was thinking, "He's about to crush this test!"

Trisha pointed to a series of letters, and Jay had to accurately identify them. First, she pointed to the letter A and said, "Jay, what letter is this?" Jay answered, "E." She then pointed to the letter L and asked him the same question. Jay repeated: "E." Trisha gave me a look. I could not believe this was happening. After all the work we've put into this, the only answer you can give is "E"? I lightly pinched Jay's leg under the table, hoping to get him to snap out of it, but it didn't work. I'm sure he did identify some of the letters, but all I kept hearing was "E."

Trisha was still so encouraging. When she gave me that look, I knew what it meant: we needed to get it together quick, fast, and in a hurry. What amazed me, and still does to this day, is that Jay was not at all phased by the entire experience. He grabbed me and told me he was ready to go home. That was one of the longest car rides ever.

I wanted to be angry and fuss at Jay, but instead, I looked into his eyes and told him everything would be alright and that we were going to take a break and enjoy the summer. Although I did not believe what I was saying at that time, I do believe in the power of words. So if I speak it often enough, eventually, things will turn around.

Kindergarten was a familiar experience in that it was an extension to transitional kindergarten. Thankfully, Trisha kept Jay on her roster. I know she had her own personal thoughts about Jay's situation, but she made sure she remained objective and encouraging.

As we progressed through the school year, Jay was still not very communicative. We could tell that he wanted to do a good job on every assignment, but he just did not verbalize his thoughts. As a result, I felt like his spokesperson during our meetings with Trisha.

Moreover, another element was beginning to emerge: academically, Jay was not meeting kindergarten standards. Trisha and I worked on various ways to enhance his learning: simple readers, ABC Mouse, teacher-led elective classes. In the midst of all of this, Jay remained cool, calm, and collected. He was living his best life. I, on the other hand, felt that his educational experience was being ruined. I began to doubt that homeschooling had been the right decision after all.

Our season with Trisha as Jay's E.S. would end at the conclusion of the school year. She had accepted a new position in the school that would take effect the following school year. Trisha and I talked about it, and she mentioned that there was a Special Education specialist that might possibly be a good fit for Jay. I was open to the idea. I was hoping she might suggest some creative ways to help Jay blossom.

Shortly after I heard the news, I told Jay that Trisha would be assuming a new role and that he would have a different E.S. next year. I asked him if he understood, and he said, "Yes." But what happened next surprised me. For the remainder of the year, Trisha was greeted by a very chatty Jay! Oh, he had a lot to say now. I think she even received some hugs. He was like a completely different boy. I could not believe my eyes and ears. I still recall the joy in Trisha's voice as she administered the year-end assessment. Jay's score improved, and he was engaged in conversation the entire time.

As we said our goodbyes, I could see that Trisha was pleased with how the school year had ended. That made me feel better because I knew she was being honest with me. When I closed the door, Jay walked up to me and said, "How did I do, mommy?"

I remember replying: "Boy, you are something else."

Chapter 6
Here Comes the Storm

The summer leading up to first grade was wonderful. Jay's personality was really starting to emerge. He loved to tell stories and to make me laugh. His confidence was growing as well. It was so refreshing to see Jay initiate interaction with other children. This alone made me feel better about navigating through these choppy homeschooling waters. However, I wish I'd felt more confident about my ability to teach Jay. In fact I felt quite the opposite. But in my mind, regardless of how I felt, my focus was solely on making sure Jay received all the educational support he needed.

I truly went overboard with all my preparations. Jay had two to three designated learning spaces throughout the house. We had books galore, workbooks, supplies. You name it; we had it. I was going to make sure that my son's new Educational Specialist knew we meant business. Soon our entire house looked like a learning center. But as wonderful as that was (or so I thought), our actual living space felt increasingly smaller. I remember telling my mother that we were outgrowing our home. I did not realize that I was actually creating change with the very words that I spoke.

The day arrived for Jay and I to meet his new specialist, Katie, an E.S. in Special Education, and I was excited to learn as much as I could from her about which teaching methods I could incorporate into my own day-to-day teaching.

Katie and I kept the same meeting arrangement I had had with Trisha: we would meet at my parents' home. The meetings with Katie were pleasant. She had a calming quality about her toward which Jay gravitated. He enjoyed his time with "Ms. Katie." I soon discovered that Katie and I were similar in that we thrive better with some sort of structure in place. I had initially hoped I could lean on her for more creative ways to teach children, but she was helpful to us in other ways.

I believe that God allowed Katie and my family to cross paths because she was going to play a pivotal role in Jay's education, and in turn, Jay and I were going to have an impact on how she would work with children in the future. As I recall, Jay was the first student on her roster with a speech IEP. Her experience up to that point had been exclusively with students with an academic IEP, which may or may not include speech. So this was not only a new experience for our family but her as well.

The first half of first grade was very exciting for Jay and overwhelming at the same time. He had always been a pretty mellow boy who enjoys the simple things in life, while I can be something of an overachiever. Unfortunately, that is how I planned his schedule: as if I were the one in school. I remember placing Jay in Spanish immersion class. My mother laughed at me and said, "He has to master the English language first!" To Jay's credit, he did well in Spanish, and I only withdrew him because the class was too far along by the time he joined. Jay was a trooper: whatever adventure I planned, he was along for the ride.

Mid-year, our lives began to change. I received a call from my client and could tell by his voice the news was not good. He proceeded to inform me that he would be scaling back and would need to reduce my billable hours. I was concerned, as I was the sole provider, but not worried. I may not have had the strongest faith in other areas of my life, but I did not lack faith when it came to making money.

So I figured God had something else lined up for me and that I just needed to be in the right place at the right time. I tried my best to focus on homeschooling Jay, but now I would have to keep a roof over our heads. So I hired a tutor to work with Jay every day on the core subjects: Math, Language, Reading. I was still responsible for going through Jay's lessons with him, but the tutor did most of the heavy lifting. In the evenings, I networked as much as I could.

May came and went; so did June, July, and August. Nothing changed financially. I felt like my situation was beginning to spin out of control. In the past, God would miraculously open doors of opportunity for me — but this felt different: it felt bigger than me. And so, for the first time in many years, I had no plan of action. I was completely at God's mercy. Quite frankly, that felt terrible. The Lord knows His children, and He knows I am more at peace when I feel I have some sort of control over things. However, this time, He put me not in the passenger seat but in the back seat and pushed the child-proof lock button. There was no getting out of this one. He wanted me to yield to His way.

Just before my son's birthday in October, it became clear to me that we were going to have to move. Unfortunately,

I was not able to secure another contract: I was completely devastated. What I did not know is that God placed it in my mother's heart to ask my stepfather if Jay and I could move in with them. He said yes.

My parents live in a beautiful home, and my mother is very meticulous. Her formal dining room looks like a showcase room right out of *Better Homes and Gardens*. It is one thing to have a six-year-old visit your home; it is another thing altogether to have a six-year-old *live* in your home.

Thus in December 2015, Jay and I packed up and moved to the Central Valley. It felt unreal. Little did I know that God had some divine connections waiting for Jay.

Chapter 7
Just Give Us a Little More Time

I would be lying if I told you that Jay and I adjusted well in the Central Valley. But God bless my parents: there was more than enough room for all of us. However, I am extremely independent, and the thought of not having a home of my own did not sit well. Jay had regressed a little. I think he was upset with me for taking him away from the only home he had ever known and from his friends. It seemed as if we were both mourning what we had lost. To help us feel better, we returned to our favorite restaurants and had many play dates with neighborhood friends.

During Jay's second-grade year, Katie, his Educational Specialist, informed me that he had a low score on the i-Ready assessment and therefore needed intervention. This consisted in selecting one school-approved online tool that Jay would work on at least forty-five minutes every day, after which he would be evaluated during each learning period meeting to measure his progress. At first, I resisted because I felt that Jay just needed more time. Katie and I went back and forth on the issue, and I even spoke to her director. It may sound silly, but I did not want the school to open a file on my son to label him.

The school and I eventually came to a consensus, and I allowed Jay to select the online intervention tool he preferred. We did what the school requested, but in the back of my mind, I kept thinking that it is not the school's job to make sure my son succeeds: it's mine. As wonderful and kind as Katie was, she could only do so much for us. The school has its rules, and there were boxes that needed to be checked off for each student. If Jay did not fit into a particular box, the school would make adjustments to fit him into one of those categories. The box that I could see Katie wanting to put Jay into was Special Education.

In my opinion, our family was something of a challenge for Katie because she would have related to Jay more easily had there been an academic IEP that served as a guide. The IEP that Jay had in place, however, was for speech only, so there was a delicate balance involved in helping a child who may not be at grade level and with no education plan of specific steps to achieve that goal. Also, I was probably different from any parent Katie had dealt with before, as I served as Jay's gatekeeper. Katie knew she could tell me about any observations she made as well as any suggestions regarding Jay's progress or even lack thereof. However, that information stopped with me and would not be filtered down to Jay.

Katie wanted to have Jay evaluated for a possible learning disability. She broached the topic gently by sharing that if Jay did have a learning disability, he would have access to many more services. By the look on my face, she could tell I was not open to it. Jay's scores were driving her decision, and I completely understood that, but I have a special connection with my son and just did not feel that this was the right course of action for him.

There were days when I doubted myself. However, God always brings clarity to a situation. To help Jay improve his test scores, I contacted a local tutoring company, and they sent one of their top tutors. I don't recall her name, but I do remember her presence. She walked into our home with such confidence and had a very professional demeanor. I was impressed. We sat down, and she gave me an overview of her organization and how they worked with a new student. She would give Jay a brief assessment to evaluate how best to assist him in reaching his academic goals. As soon as she said that, I thought, "Here we go again with another assessment...."

Once the tutor completed the assessment, she said she was going to call her director. I thought, "Well, that can't be good." Then I heard something that honestly shocked me. "I think we have a gifted learner here," she told the director. I was stunned. Did she really say what I thought she said? Up to this point on paper, Jay's scores were saying just the opposite! As soon as the tutor ended her call, I asked her, "How did my son do on the assessment?" She replied: "Your son did well. He shows signs of being a gifted learner." I could hardly maintain my composure because I was filled with such joy. I thanked her for her time and let her know we would be in touch soon.

As soon as I closed the door, I grabbed Jay and gave him a big hug and kiss. I know he thought I was crazy. God had just given me the confirmation I needed to know how to move forward with Jay. In the midst of all we had gone through, this news put the wind back in my sails.

That day my way became crystal clear. As much as I wanted to grow my business, my son needed me to be by his side. God knew that had we stayed in our home, I would have outsourced teaching my son to a teacher (which I tried) and would have focused almost exclusively on my business. God wanted me to walk through this season beside Jay. Tutors would only be used as a checks and balance to make sure Jay received the support he needed.

As I focused on my son and his needs, the Lord sent some unique opportunities for me to earn money. I recall working on a small project for an international best-selling author. The project lasted only about three weeks, but we were able to use the money for a wonderful Christmas. I participated in focus groups, paid panel discussions, and other opportunities that came my way. During this season, God did not give me more than enough: he literally gave me what we needed each day. This season, I admit, was a very humbling time in my life. In hindsight, God was not only doing a work in Jay's life but in my life as well.

I never told Katie that Jay had shown signs of being a gifted learner because I understood that in her mind, his scores would need to reflect that. However, I was determined to find the right formula to unlock Jay's abilities on my own.

I wish I could tell you that Jay soared academically, but things played out differently. Jay's scores remained below grade level in the second grade through the first half of fourth grade. He was growing academically, but the learning gap was widening each year, making it a challenge for him to catch up. Jay worked so hard. He really wanted to succeed, and Katie could see that. She would always tell me, "You're doing a great job, mom!" Katie knew how invested I was, and I think that is why she was so flexible with us. She was always open to hearing my ideas about Jay's education.

Unfortunately, the tension in the house between Jay and I started to develop. He was growing tired of always being evaluated, and I was weary because we were not seeing substantial results. There were times I wanted to quit and put Jay back in school, but how could I do that to him, especially now? When it came to school, I was always strict with Jay, but now my teaching was also filled with frustration and anger. We both needed something to change.

In March of Jay's fourth-grade year, we faced a crossroads. Every year, I met with Katie, Jay's Educational Specialist, his Speech Therapist, and his lead facilitator to go over Jay's goals for the school year and develop goals for the next one. Normally Katie would lead the discussion with her report of Jay's progress and challenges throughout the year. That included the results of the California Assessment of Student Performance and Progress (CAASPP) state-mandated test of the previous year. The speech therapist would discuss her goals and the progress made, and from there, we would go over Jay's academic plan for the upcoming year.

Although I had become accustomed to the routine nature of these meetings, this year, the tone was different. Jay would be going into the fifth grade and was still performing below grade level. The elephant in the room was whether he should be evaluated for a learning disability. No one verbalized this to me directly, but I could tell by the lead facilitator's tone. In fact I remember hearing this: "If Jay's scores do not improve, he will just die in fifth grade, with the rigorous work he will be expected to do." I could not believe she had said that out loud. Instead of getting upset, however, I told them if Jay's scores had not improved by the time we met the following March, I would agree to have him evaluated.

I knew Jay, and I needed some space when it came to his schooling. Maybe I was too close to the situation to see things clearly? I had no answers at this point, but I did know that Jay needed someone other than myself to help him prepare for the CAASPP test at the end of the school year.

Based upon a friend's recommendation, Jay began meeting with a tutor near our home in a one-person office converted into a classroom. Jay and I enjoyed it. The first ten minutes was a Bible lesson, and the remainder of the lesson was prepping for the CAASPP test. Jay was tutored four days a week. For the first two months, things went well, but then I noticed that both Jay and his tutor seemed to be losing interest in working together. They were both respectful to each other, but Jay would just drift off halfway through the session, and sometimes I caught the tutor falling asleep as Jay was completing a problem on the chalkboard. Needless to say, I politely discontinued these tutoring sessions.

When Jay was nearing the end of fourth grade, I asked him to be honest: did he still want me to be his teacher? He looked at me and said, "Not really." I looked at him and said, "Neither do I." Then I had a thought. I asked Jay how he would feel about taking live core courses through the charter school next year. He replied, "Okay, mom."

Back to the drawing board, we went.

Chapter 8
Our Breakthrough Is Here!

During the summer months, I would usually have Jay work on specific academic skills to fill in some learning gaps. However, the summer after fourth grade, Jay and I both needed a break from the hustle and bustle of school. We actually disengaged for the entire summer. It was such a wonderful feeling just being Jay's mom again. So often, the lines had gotten blurred between my role as his mother and my role as his teacher. At the beginning of this journey, I had tried to be really conscious of those two roles, but by third grade, Jay knew to expect the unexpected. Some days I wore my mom hat, other days, my teacher hat, and on some days, it was a combination of both. That summer, I knew that Jay just needed me to be his mom.

After our well-rested summer, the big day arrived to register Jay for his online classes. I spoke with Katie and let her know that I wanted to enroll him in the following courses: Math 5 and Language Arts 5. Science and Social Studies was not available at that time, so I placed Jay in Outschool classes. Katie and I both felt that although Jay had a steep learning curve, this experience would be good for him. And was it ever!

It took Jay a couple of weeks to get acclimated to his classes. After that, he was off and running. I think the highlight of each class for him was reading his peers' comments in the chat. Up to this point, Jay had not experienced various classroom student types: the comic, the storyteller, the instigator, the model student. Now, at some point during each class, I would hear Jay say, "Mom, you have to read this!"

Katie and I were both delightfully surprised at how well Jay was doing in his classes. We still had some work to do in the background to help Jay continue having a positive experience in his classes, and there were still some math and reading gaps that the charter school had identified. As I knew Jay was bored with the online intervention tools, I enrolled him in a Developmental Math class, leaving Reading as the only subject that would require the intervention tool. Separate from the school, I also used Read Naturally to assist with the novel reading he would be doing in Language Arts 5.

For the first time, I felt as if we had found the right mix for Jay to blossom. Katie even started to believe we were on the right track. My interactions with her were now lighter, and she no longer suggested having Jay evaluated for a learning disability. I always knew Jay had capabilities; I just could not tell when he would begin to blossom. That 'when' was the most difficult part because I knew the school wanted to see results.

In November of Jay's fifth-grade year (2019), all students at the charter school had to take a Fall/Winter assessment to see how they were progressing and identify any learning gaps. The morning of Jay's assessment, we were completely calm; for the first time, I was not obsessing about how well he would do. I remember driving him to the local library, where the assessment would be administered. When we stepped into the library, there were kids everywhere. I wondered how on earth Jay would be able to concentrate. After walking around for a few minutes, we spotted Katie. We chatted for a few minutes, and then I ran some errands for a couple of hours while Jay took the assessment. When I picked him up afterward, he really did not want to talk about it; he was just ready to go home. I said no more, and we went home and ate dinner.

In January 2020, Katie sent me Jay's assessment results from November. Usually, I would take a moment to mentally prepare myself before reading that email. This time I opened the email immediately. As soon as I saw Jay's results, I ran into his room and hugged him. I know he thought I was crazy. Tears filled my eyes, and all I could think of was, "Our breakthrough is here!"

There is something to be said for staying true to what you believe God is telling you to do. Here are screenshots of my son's scores in Language Arts and Math.

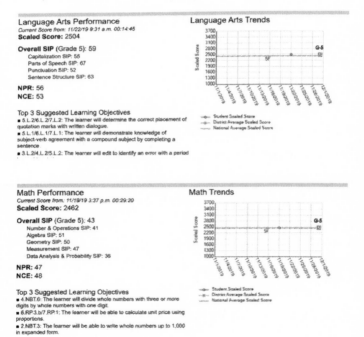

Our annual IEP meeting with the charter school staff had a much different tone than last year's meeting. The focus was no longer on goals to help Jay bridge the learning gap but on supporting his academic growth so he could continue to thrive. That was music to my ears.

In March 2020, our world changed radically as a result of COVID-19. We were fortunate that the charter school was already a virtual institution, so the students did not experience a lapse in instruction. Mentally, however, completing the remainder of the school year was very challenging. Nevertheless, I appreciated how patient the teachers were with all of their students during that difficult time.

At one of our final learning period meetings, Katie informed me that she would be retiring at the end of the school year. It was hard to believe that she has been with us since Jay's first-grade year. We had been through so much together, and I feel that God had selected Katie to help us navigate through this challenging season in Jay's academic life.

I gave Jay his space over the summer and allowed him to process what was going on in the world as best he could. His passion is basketball, so he would practice his drills either at the park or at the hoop in front of our house.

At the beginning of his sixth-grade year, Jay took a diagnostic assessment to determine if he would require intervention. From second through fifth grades, Jay's school year had included some sort of online intervention. Would it be the same this year?

As a result of all his hard work and thanks to the proverbial village we were fortunate to have around us, Jay exceeded all our expectations: for the first time, he did not need an intervention tool. He could experience the school year in a new way. It was almost as if he had been waiting for us to give him some breathing room so he could blossom.

Below are Jay's end of sixth-grade i-Ready diagnostic scores, along with his report card and grade percentages:

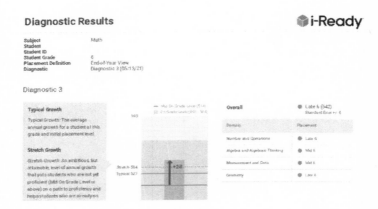

Diagnostic Results

i-Ready

Subject: Reading
Student:
Student ID:
Student Grade: 6
Placement Definition: End-of-Year View
Diagnostic: Diagnostic 3 (04/30/23)

Diagnostic 3

Typical Growth

Typical Growth: The average annual growth for a student at this grade and initial placement level.

Stretch Growth

Stretch Growth: An ambitious, but attainable, level of annual growth that puts students who are not yet proficient (Mid On Grade Level or above) on a path to proficiency and helps students who are already on track for proficiency to achieve or maintain advanced proficiency levels.

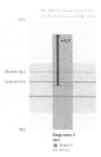

Overall Grade 5 (685)
Standard Error +/- 15

Domain	Placement
Phonological Awareness*	Tested Out
Phonics*	Tested Out
High-Frequency Words*	Tested Out
Vocabulary	Grade 5
Comprehension: Literature	Grade 5
Comprehension: Informational Text	Grade 7

* Results below Grade levels

Connecting Waters Charter School
Report Card

Student: Student ID:
Teacher: Teacher ID:
Year *(Effective Date)*: 2020 - 2021 (05/21/2021)   Grade: 6

Subject	Semester 2 (Spring)		
	Mark	**Comments**	
6th Grade Science	E		
English Language Arts 6	E		
Math-6	E	J	applies himself and showed learning and discipline in my math class.
PE-6	E		
Social Studies-6	E		

Completion
This student has (completed/not completed) _____ all course work for grade ___ and (has/has not) been promoted to grade ___.

Courses I'm Taking

CP5002 Math 6
94.63%

CP 1033.1 Novel Explorations
100%

CP 1000 English 6
93.27%

CP6024 Science 6
101.09%

To say I was proud of Jay would be an understatement. In hindsight, I could see God's hand at work in every step of this long and challenging process. I still chuckle when I see Jay's report card. Maybe he was sending me a message in kindergarten when he answered all the assessment questions with the letter E.

Reflection

PART III

Chapter 9
Homeschooling From Jay's Perspective

As I reflect on this experience thus far, all of its ups and downs, highs and lows, the person who was most affected in this process is my son. And so, I feel it would be instructive to hear directly from Jay. We sat down and had a brief chat about his homeschool experience up to this point. Below is our dialogue.

Teressa: Hello son, how are you?

Jay: I'm good, how are you?

Teressa: I am doing well, thank you. I figured that at this point in the book, readers might benefit from hearing directly from you. Do you mind if I ask you some questions?

Jay: No, I don't mind.

Teressa: Before we get started, please tell readers how old you are and what grade you are going into.

Jay: I am 12 years old, and I am going into the 7th grade.

Teressa: Okay, so here is the first question. What is your favorite subject, and why?

Jay: My favorite subject is Math because I'm really good at it.

Teressa: Do you feel you are academically prepared for 7th grade?

Jay: Yes, I do.

Teressa: In general, what do you like about homeschooling?

Jay: I like how short the sessions are, so I can continue with my other activities.

Teressa: What is it that you like the least about homeschooling?

Jay: Sometimes I don't really like how busy it gets because I want to play my games. I feel it's rewarding, though.

Teressa: How did you feel about Mommy teaching you? Don't worry; you can be honest!

Jay: I felt you did a pretty good job with teaching me some stuff. It wasn't a whole lot, but you still did alright.

Teressa: How did you feel about having to take the monthly assessments each time you met with Ms. Katie during your learning period meetings?

Jay: Sometimes I felt nervous. Other times I felt like I could do it. Also, my most favorite part about it was reading to see how I improved over one month.

Teressa: When I told someone I was homeschooling you, usually the first thing I would hear was 'Your son needs to socialize more.' Do you feel that you have enough social activities?

Jay: Yes, I socialize with my basketball friends. I used to make friends out at the playground, but now it's on the basketball court.

Teressa: What advice would you like to give to parents who are homeschooling or would like to homeschool?

Jay: First, be patient with your children. Don't get so frustrated. Do not teach subjects the way you were taught as a kid because it may not be the right way.

Teressa: What would you like to say to children who are being homeschooled?

Jay: Be nice to your parents when you're being homeschooled. Try to figure out some of the problems on your own.

Teressa: Okay, last question. Do your friends who are

not homeschooled treat you differently because you are homeschooled?

Jay: No, my friends do not treat me differently. They treat me the same, and they say I am lucky!

Teressa: Those are all of the questions I had. Thank you for your time, son. I love you.

Jay: And I love you, mom.

Chapter 10

My Tips to Help Families Homeschool Their Children

I have always believed that God allows us to have certain experiences so that we can be a blessing to others. I am by no means an expert at homeschooling, but I would be remiss if I did not share some information that helped me support my son up to this point. Below are some of the strategies I practiced during each school year.

It is important to include your child in their education planning process

I found that I really got my son's buy-in when I asked for his input and placed him in the driver's seat. I had to learn that it is important to allow children to have control over their learning experience. When I put this into practice, Jay became less resistant.

Know your child's teacher(s) and understand the expectations of distance learning

Whether you homeschool like myself or are currently distance learning, your child's teacher or school should provide each family with some guidance on what is reasonable online learning per day. Additionally, it is important to understand the homework policies and the teachers' expectations for their students.

Establish a designated learning space with minimal distractions

This is key. It is important, when possible, to reduce distractions when your child is completing schoolwork or attending an online class. This includes eliminating excess noise as well as providing an uncluttered workspace. A designated workspace will help put your child in the mindset to work.

Encourage movement

My child is very energetic, so I have a mini-basketball hoop outside our office. When he gets overwhelmed or needs to burn some energy, he shoots a few hoops.

Use a checklist for focus

This is for some children who may need help with focusing, or even adults like me. To keep Jay and I on track with his schedule and tasks, I created a checklist and placed it right outside the office door. As we went throughout the day and he completed a task, he would check that item off as being completed.

Adjust the schedule as needed

I cannot begin to tell you how many times we revised our schedule. Pre-live classes, if I sensed that Jay was getting frustrated, I would stop the lesson and move on to another subject. Then later in the day, I would try to re-teach the subject that had frustrated Jay earlier. With live classes, I would move the homework schedule around. As Jay got older, I found he wanted to tackle the more difficult homework first.

Give your child and yourself a break

At the outset of my homeschooling journey, I used to try to push through teaching a subject, even if Jay was crying or I was frustrated. Predictably, that did not work out. So I had to give myself permission to take a break and excuse myself if I needed to. Above all, I wanted Jay to enjoy the learning process, and that clearly was not happening when he was crying. If things were not going well and Jay was exhausted, I would stop the lesson for the day and try again the next day.

Utilize non-traditional tools to teach concepts

My son is a visual learner, so if a concept is not clear to him, I will use tools such as Brainpop, Khan Academy, YouTube mini-lessons, and/or Outschool until I find what works for him.

Praise their work and their efforts

This strategy took me some time to put into practice. I am so results-driven and would focus on the areas Jay needed to improve upon with his studies that I did not realize I was draining him. Once I started acknowledging Jay's hard work, he was motivated to accomplish even more.

Empower your children by letting them teach you concepts

I find that this can be a real confidence booster for my son. Jay really excels in math, but we would always disagree on the approach to solving a math problem. So a simple homework assignment would take hours. Katie suggested letting Jay teach me the math concepts, and this actually worked. I found that when Jay was walking me through the steps while solving a problem, this gave me insight into his level of understanding.

Be gentle with yourself and with your child

If nothing else, please remember there is no one way to homeschool. There is a fine line between being a parent and being a home educator. If you are anything like me, that line gets crossed quite a bit. Each child has a different learning style, and it will take time to discover what works best for your family.

Find a homeschooling mentor

My son and I are members of a most amazing homeschooling group. We know parents who have successfully homeschooled their children, and they are now thriving in college. It is important to surround yourself with others who have been where you are going.

Build your child's learning experience around their passion

Jay has a passion for basketball. For him, it's more than just playing basketball. He literally has some sort of basketball commentary playing in the background, whether he is playing a game or doing homework. I try as much as possible to select his class times around his basketball practice and training schedule. I even used basketball to teach math lessons!

Conclusion

PART IV

Chapter 11
On the Move

As I write this final chapter, Jay is on the eve of turning thirteen. When I look into his eyes, I feel that everything we went through to reach this point was more than worth it. Jay is my gift from God, and I am a better human being because of him.

The title of this chapter is 'On the Move.' Throughout this process, I have learned to be sensitive when God is prompting me to make a change. Jay's confidence has grown so much — and so has mine. After much prayer, moving forward, I have decided to exclusively homeschool Jay without the assistance of the charter school. I know that with the help of our village, I can continue to provide a supportive environment for Jay to thrive in. I am truly excited about what is to come.

I hope our story has encouraged you to continue to take those steps forward and to stand firm in what you believe. Yes, there will be obstacles, and there will be opposition from those who do not understand. But at the end of the day, God did not speak to others: He spoke to you. And if He spoke to you, He will provide you with all the resources you need and with people to walk alongside you on your journey.

He did so with me, and for that, I and my son Jay remain eternally grateful.

Made in the USA
Middletown, DE
22 December 2021

56272721R00050